KATE RIGGS

grow with me

FROG

CREATIVE EDUCATION

Published by Creative Education
P.O. Box 227, Mankato, Minnesota 56002
Creative Education is an imprint of
The Creative Company
www.thecreativecompany.us

Design and production by Ellen Huber
Art direction by Rita Marshall
Printed in the United States of America

Photographs by Alamy (Danita Delimont, Image
Quest Marine, Prisma Bildagentur AG, Kevin
Schafer), Bigstock (alptraum, odvdveer), Biosphoto
(Renaud Fulconis), Getty Images (Michael Dunning,
George Grall/National Geographic, Gary Mezaros/
Visuals Unlimited, Inc.), iStockphoto (Antagain,
Norbert Bieberstein, Adam Gryko, Jiří Hodeček,
malerapaso, Lee Pettet), Photo Researchers (Dante
Fenolio), Photolibrary (Oxford Scientific), Shutterstock
(hagit berkovich), SuperStock (Flirt, imagebroker.net,
Minden Pictures), Veer (kikkerdirk, stevebyland)

Library of Congress Cataloging-in-Publication Data
Riggs, Kate.
Frog / Kate Riggs.
p. cm. — (Grow with me)
Includes bibliographical references and index.
Summary: An exploration of the life cycle and life
span of frogs, using up-close photographs and step-
by-step text to follow a frog's growth process from egg
to tadpole to froglet to mature amphibian.

ISBN 978-1-60818-216-9
1. Frogs—Life cycles—Juvenile literature. I. Title.
QL668.E2R53 2012
597.8'9—dc23   2011040499

First Edition
9 8 7 6 5 4 3 2 1

TABLE OF CONTENTS

Frogs are amphibians (*am-FIH-bee-enz*). Amphibians can live in fresh water and on land. Frogs have short bodies, long legs, webbed or sticky feet, and large eyes. They do not have tails.

4

Frogs live in or near ponds, lakes, or rivers. They like living in warm places such as **tropical rainforests**. A few kinds of frogs live in dry deserts or very cold places. They bury themselves underground when it is too hot or cold. There are more than 4,000 frog **species** around the world.

Many tree frog
species live in
forests all across
South America.

5

⑥ Frogs spend a lot of time in water. Their eyes and nose are on top of their head. This lets them see and breathe when their bodies are mostly underwater.

Frogs do not need to drink water because their skin soaks it up. They are meat-eaters, even though they do not have teeth. Frogs like to eat **insects** and worms.

Insects such as dragonflies are favorite foods for frogs in lakes and ponds.

7

The red-eyed tree frog
lays its eggs under
leaves in Costa Rica.

8

A mother frog usually lays her eggs in water. Some frogs lay eggs on plant leaves above a lake or river. A female frog can lay hundreds or thousands of eggs at a time!

The eggs float on the water and are called a frogspawn (*FROG-spon*). They are surrounded by a clear jelly. Some frog eggs are brown or black. The dark color helps the eggs absorb heat from the sun. If the eggs get too cold, they will not survive.

9

The small black dots inside the frogspawn will soon turn into tadpoles.

When tree frogs' eggs hatch, tadpoles drop into the water below the leaf.

(10) As soon as it is laid, the egg starts to change. Inside, a frog **larva** called a tadpole is growing. When it is in the egg, the tadpole is known as an **embryo** (*EM-bree-oh*).

The egg hatches after about a week, and a tadpole swims out. The tadpole's body is shaped like a chicken egg. It has a mouth and a long, flat tail that is good for swimming. Tadpoles live only in the water. They have **gills** so they can breathe.

Tadpoles generally like to swim in warm water that is not too deep.

11

Tadpoles keep their mouths open to catch floating bits of food.

The tadpoles feed on plants such as algae (*AL-gee*). They do not have teeth, but some tadpoles can still eat insects. Tadpoles even eat each other sometimes!

Tadpoles may be eaten by many **predators**. Fish, lizards called newts, and some birds like to eat tadpoles. Some tadpoles are **poisonous**. Other animals stay away from them.

13

After two or three months, a tadpole is ready to start changing into an adult frog. Some tadpoles stay just as they are over the winter. But most change into frogs by summer.

14

A tadpole goes through a process of change called metamorphosis (*met-ah-MORE-foh-sis*). This word means "change shape."

This frog from Australia started as a brown tadpole and is changing into a green adult.

15

Frog metamorphosis takes about three weeks. In that time, a tadpole starts to look like a frog. It grows front legs. Its **jaw** gets bigger. Its eyes grow larger and move to the top of the head. Then its skin gets thicker, too.

16

Twelve weeks after it hatched from its egg,
a tadpole looks like a small frog with a tail.
It is now called a froglet.

The common frog
stops eating for a while
when it first changes
into a froglet.

17

Between 12 and 16 weeks after hatching, the froglet's tail gets smaller. Its back legs grow longer. It can breathe air using its lungs instead of gills.

At last, the tail disappears. The froglet is now a frog. It is ready to leave the water as an adult. Adult frogs come in many different colors. Most are brown, gray, or green. Some are bright colors such as red or yellow. Some frogs can change color. They do this to blend in with the things around them or to keep from getting too hot or cold.

Frogs cannot see color. Their eyes see only in black and white.

18

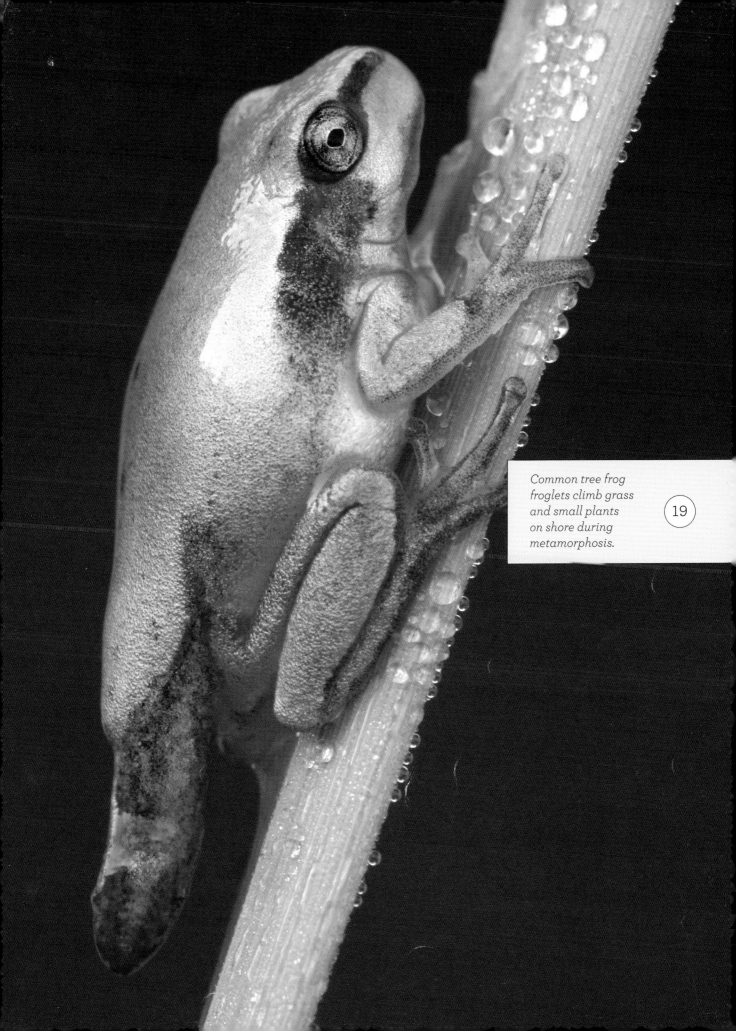

Common tree frog froglets climb grass and small plants on shore during metamorphosis.

19

Young adult frogs find new homes on land. Most stay close to the water. They eat small animals and fish. Some use their long, sticky tongues to catch bugs and other fast **prey**.

20

Many animals like to eat frogs. Big fish, snakes, birds, foxes, and other predators hunt frogs. In some places, people catch frogs to eat their legs, too.

Even fast-flying moths are no match for a frog's sticky tongue.

21

Most frogs can live between 4 and 15 years, if they don't get eaten. Some kinds of frogs in **captivity** have lived as long as 40 years.

Frogs that hatched in the spring become adults in the fall. In places where winters bring cold weather, frogs may **hibernate**. Frogs are full-grown, or mature, after a few months or a couple of years. When they are mature, they find mates.

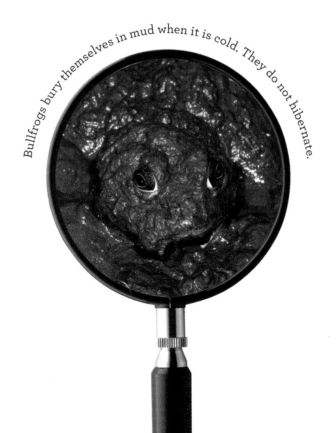

Bullfrogs bury themselves in mud when it is cold. They do not hibernate.

Some frog mates
stay together after
the female lays eggs.
But most do not.

23

Some frogs make calls
to warn others that
rain is coming or
to mark their territory.

24

Male marsh frogs blow their vocal sacs like bubbles to get a female's attention.

Frogs usually mate in the spring. Male frogs call out to females to let them know they are ready to mate. Then the females call back. Every frog species has a different call.

25

The frog's mouth stays closed when it calls. Air passes through a part of the throat called the larynx (*LARE-inks*). The sound of the call is made louder by pouches of skin under the throat called vocal sacs. Some frogs' calls are so loud they can be heard up to a mile (1.6 km) away!

After frogs mate, female frogs lay their eggs right away. If the eggs are not laid in water, the male and female frogs will stay with the eggs to protect them.

Some frogs lay their eggs on the floor of the rainforest. After the eggs hatch, one of the parents carries the tadpoles on his or her back to a big plant that collects water. The tadpoles will grow in that small pool of water.

26

Frogs that live in trees have sticky pads on their toes to help them climb.

This male golden poison dart frog is carrying his tadpoles on his back.

28 *Wood frogs lay their eggs in pools of water where no fish live.*

Frogs mate every year so the females can keep laying eggs. Females lay as many eggs as they can before they die. Every egg has a chance to become a tadpole. And after a tadpole loses its tail, it will turn into a croaking frog.

The biggest frog in the world, the goliath frog, is 12 inches (30 cm) long.

The frog lays her eggs 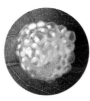 in the water or on a plant.

An embryo begins growing in the egg.

The embryo (called a tadpole) hatches from the egg in a week.

The tadpole begins the process of metamorphosis after 8 or 12 weeks.

30

The tadpole becomes a froglet when it is 11 to 15 weeks old.

Sixteen weeks after hatching, the froglet leaves the water.

The young adult frog matures for 9 months to 2 years.

At around 2 years old, the frog begins mating.

After 2 to 13 more years, the frog dies.

captivity: *held in a cage or other place not in the wild*

embryo: *an offspring that has not hatched out of an egg yet*

gills: *openings in a tadpole's skin that let it get air out of water*

hibernate: *to spend the winter sleeping or not moving around much*

insects: *animals that have six legs and one or two pairs of wings*

jaw: *the bony structure of the mouth*

larva: *the form a frog takes after it hatches but before it has legs; "larvae" is the word for more than one larva*

poisonous: *causing death or illness*

predators: *animals that kill and eat other animals*

prey: *animals that are killed and eaten by other animals*

species: *groups of living things that are closely related*

tropical rainforests: *hot and wet places where many plants grow; they are found in the hottest parts of the world*

31

WEB SITES

Amphibians Preschool Crafts and Activities
http://www.first-school.ws/theme/animals/amphibians.htm
Learn more about frogs and make frogs of your own.

Printable Frog Activities for Kids
**http://www.printactivities.com/Theme-Printables/
Frog-Printables.html**
Print out frog puzzles and coloring pages.

READ MORE

Arnosky, Jim. *All about Frogs.*
New York: Scholastic, 2002.

Moffett, Mark. *Face to Face with Frogs.*
Washington, D.C.: National Geographic, 2008.

32

INDEX